The Year of the Poet

May 2014

The Poetry Posse

inner child press, ltd.

The Poetry Posse

Jamie Bond

Gail Weston Shazor

Albert 'Infinite' Carrasco

Siddartha Beth Pierce

Janet P. Caldwell

June 'Bugg' Barefield

Debbie M. Allen

Tony Henninger

Joe DaVerbal Minddancer

Robert Gibbons

Neetu Wali

Shareef Abdur – Rasheed

Kimberly Burnham

William S. Peters, Sr.

General Information

The Year of the Poet
May Edition

The Poetry Posse

1st Edition : 2014

Publisher Information

1st Edition : Inner Child Press :
intouch@innerchildpress.com
www.innerchildpress.com

ISBN-13 : 978-0692213261 (Inner Child Press, Ltd.)
ISBN-10 : 0692213260

$ 12.99

poetry is . . .
India INK

Dedication

This Book is dedicated to

Poetry

&

the Spirit

of our Everlasting Muse.

Poets . . .
sowing seeds in the
Conscious Garden of Life,
that those who have yet to come
may enjoy the Flowers.

Foreword

Dear Friend,

I am the Father of 11 Children, and the Grand Father of 8 more, so when i consider the plight of our children in our world today, i am deeply concerned about not only their well being, but their happiness. I think the world today steals the precious moments of childhood in so many ways with all the Social Issues, Abuse, and Molestation that can potentially affect our treasures. This for me is very saddening, for i had the opportunity to be a Child in the purest of senses.

Perhaps we can attribute our own awareness to the instantaneousness of our modern day world system of communication with such things as the Internet, Tablets and Smart Phone. If nothing else our awareness of the challenges that face our children and that of the future generations to come becomes that more poignant.

This month we at The Year of the Poet, for the first time selected a theme for our monthly offering of May 2014. Our theme is simply Our Children. We are addressing via our individual perspectives the challenges they face in our 'modern' day society. Our aim si simply to elevate the awareness and perhaps motivate others to action. Yes, we must change, and that is the focus of our works as conscious Human Beings and Conscious Poets. There are some great minds contained in this month's offering and we do hope not only do you enjoy our work, but that you pass it on.

All of our Books are available for a Free Download at the Inner Child Press Web Site.

http://www.innerchildpress.com/the-year-of-the-poet.php

Feel free to share our works and "Pay It Forward"

Print copies are available direct for just $5.00.

Thank you

Bless Up

bill

Thank God for Poetry
otherwise
we would have a problem !

~ wsp

Preface

What is the Year of the Poet?

The year of the poet is a one of a kind wonderful collaborative cognizant commitment offered as a free download and a low cost book form by 14 dedicated poets being published once a month for an entire year of 2014.

The reason we created it is because statically they say that the average Author will publish maybe one book a year. The more productive writers, perhaps a few, and yet the average reader can read a typical novel in somewhere between 2 hours and 3 days. Statistics also say, the average person will read about 6-7 books a year.

This was the conversation that sparked 'just bill' and I to consider and thus commit to publish a book a month for the entire year of 2014. This was never about who is the best or better than anyone else as far as their writing. This was to ensure that we exceeded the mundane statistics of being ordinary. We are not doing it for the fame; WE are doing it to sharpen our pens with devotion.

As you read the lineup, it will give you frissons to know that each one of the Writers on this team despite their location, culture, political and religious beliefs; despite what's going on in each of their personal lives are dedicated to bringing this into fruition and thus creating history.

Ladies and Gentlemen . . .

This is simply and intricately historic. Sometimes theme based as a collective awareness… What else could we possibly call it besides, The Year Of The Poet? Look at the elite pens on this roll call The Poetry Posse that are self-conscious and unselfishly committed to raising the bar within. This is a task and vision that we have under taken to add to our poetic resume as well as share our offerings with you . . .

You get the best of our ink for FREE and We are delighted to be read.

We All Win!

Remain empowered and inspired Enjoy;

Jamie Bond

Table of Contents

The Poetry Posse

Table of Contents . . . *continued*

Poets, Writers . . . know that we are the enchanting magicians that nourishes the seeds of dreams and thoughts . . . it is our words that entice the hearts and minds of others to believe there is something grand about the possibilities that life has to offer and our words tease it forth into action . . . for you are the Poet, the Writer to whom the Gift of Words has been entrusted . . .

~ wsp

The Year of the Poet

May 2014

The Poetry Posse

inner child press, ltd.

Poetry succeeds where instruction fails.

~ wsp

Jamie
Bond

Jamie Bond aka UnMuted Ink is an authoress, radio show hostess, poetess and spoken word maven.

She is; as she says "google-able" if you type in itsbondjamiebond or unmuted ink; you'll find her on various social networks. Born and raised in Brick City aka Newark, NJ. Jamie Bond has been recognized publicly by her peers in various genres for her poetic influences. Her Poetic resume is extensive and her spoken word performances go far beyond 1,000 stage appearances globally. Best known for her networking and marketing skills; her future goals are to become more grounded as a liaison for a variety of fundraisers, activism, volunteering as an advocate as she uses her pen and voice to empower and raise the consciousness of those around her.

Her Motto

Help me to help you to help us... BUT if helping you hurts me, then I can't help you!

http://www.facebook.com/IBJB.BrickCity

Manhood ?

To the stepfather it's a malicious joke,
Mom invited him to stay without a vote
His threats make the little boy uneasy
HIS little hurt has Novocain feelings
And in her absence he molests him,
Beats him like a hazing until he's bleeding
His little body can't take this any more
His court appointed weekend now over
Terrified and afraid to tell his Daddy
He smiles, shakes hands with this predator
The Mom made this sick pervert his gatekeeper
Ill-treatment by him His cries go unheard
While his little soul begs and screams without words
BUT MOM insists that her son listen to him
Told him he must comply with the stepfather
Only feeling safe every other weekend
His would be victorious soul slaughtered
Battered assaulted like a sacrificial offering
Step Father waves dad off and locks the door
This is not love and yet… Mom never questions
His motives for wanting Quality time
With his unbiological child
Convinced that a man is being made of him
Teaching him responsibility when
Evidence of his scars are visibly seen
His naive character easily distorted
Silently wishing he were aborted
Are you going to believe him or me?
The stepfather presses the mother of him
So he's viewed as a compulsive liar
Happenstances quickly taken out of context
Everyone sees it and nobody takes notice

Hard to believe that no one knows this
Infamous for his unfathomable actions
He embezzles the preciousness of this kids
Innocence, adolescence, trust, & dreams
Being humped and beaten his existence
Becomes aimless the kid carries the sperm
Of a demon deep inside of his torn anus
Schools called with excused absences he is
Repeatedly raped Dismantled and manhandled
Being completely manipulated
For the sick sexual desires of the stepfathers
As the little boy is frightened and fighting
In the wee hours of the middle of the night
His stuffed teddy bear cries thru his one button eye
Forced to observe this assault that's everyone's fault
Unable to shut this gruesome porn flick off
There's a monster thrusting and humping on him
Nothing under the bed or in his closet
Could be a worse nightmare than this to the kid
The demonic glare of this predator
As he's raping him over again and again and again
He's told that he better not scream, better not tell,
Or else everything he loves will be killed
He's over powering in many ways
And mom refuses to notice the foul changes
The poor little kids got a busted lip,
Black eye, limping with dislocated hips
Will you look at this shit! It's ridiculous
Why does the mom keep allowing this for her kid
When the stepfather insists he's just clumsy
He's masterfully swayed her that her own
Flesh and blood is somehow uncoordinated
He's just inept it's just another accident
Older now and the light gone he doesn't care
Left for dead on the train tracks of hopeless despair

How many times did he try to plead with mom?
All The signs there refusal to pay attention?
And how many times were his pleas discredited
Avoidable but blinded by her ignorance
His obvious outbursts justifying
Many times her calling him a problem child
Continuing to get a check for him
Quick to medicate & label him a problem
His mood swings off the chain Behavioral out breaks
A developed hate for women he cannot explain
The Stepfather gives Mom an ultimatum
Make a choice…it's me or your son,
Last straw was drawn,
He's bored and the kid is getting too old for him
The alternative made made no sense to others
She said I did the best I could to raise him
As if she had limited resources
And very few options without his natural father
Too much to care for considered a handful
The natural father confused and can't do
Anything for him so he's shuffled home to home
Just needed one person to ask the right questions
One adult to appear concerned enough to save him
How dare SHE be proud and pop her collar
AS IF she deserves an award for that bullshit!!!

Transparent Gem

Behavior is more aggressive & rebellious
And it just gets worse the older she gets
Her truths are twisted and challenged
No one on her side her feelings are invalid
She's a mirror reflection of her environment
And telling an adult was never a prerequisite
Tells you she fell, Will you look at this shit!
She's damaged & weary she can't live like this
Take notice of the turmoil this is gross negligence
Made to never feel safe again always feeling depressed
Empty is the stare in the back of her eyes
Yet nobody NOBODY bothers to ask why
She's a constant casualty of a silent crime
Trapped and assaulted there's no escape from her rapist;
Unaccountable for his actions he steals her adolescence
That's her lifelong definition of love and affection
Regression in the form of avalanche
Molested in her own safe haven
She competes for affection and lowers her standards
Now fast in the ass & Lacks etiquette and manners
Her self-esteem is now stained and it just doesn't matter
He ignited the seed invoking her soul to slowly fester with cancer
And as I sit face to face and share her space
The light is gone in her eyes I see she has died
She believes her life was a message
That seems to convey no meaning
And it's your fault I couldn't resuscitate her
Since your selfishness prevented intervening
For years she'll require therapy that can't even heal her
She's still rebelling while you're in denial her tears a dried river

For so long she was a zombie just wanting her mommy
A hypothetical question undefined waiting to be answered
No more a delicate rose, nothing more than a stem with thorns
She is a survivor of a war which she never signed up for
So it's a fight she'll never win
Internally the fatality is never detected
All of this could have been prevented
Had someone played detective
Smh… Its premeditated sin against a Transparent Gem
And as a community; WE ALL allowed this to happen!

The making of a Bully

Anger inside she can’t contain
She gets humped and punch
Her little bones get crunched
The woman starves her
The man has her for lunch
The victim of a twisted system
At home she’s tormented by em
But at school she’s acting out
She senses innocence
Smells the stench on her friends
And so the bullying begins
Every boy in her little mind
Needs to be destroyed
Every girl with a toy is the target
For her hitting to be enjoyed
She terrorizes the lives
Of all the other children meanwhile
Inside she is crying out to be rescued

At home she sleeps on the floor
And gets treated less better than a dog
This is her 5th home in 13 months
Trapped in the foster care system
The new hosts tell her
That nobody's missing her
She’s beaten and mistreated
She’s only a monthly
Automatically deposited check
Her birth certificate is a receipt

She’s tired of crying
Slapped and told to stop whining
And now our society
Has a monster in their system
Of course it falls on blind eyes
As social services stay quiet
The avoidance of paperwork
…They see she’s hurt but…
Unfortunately saving her
Seems like too much work….

Gail

Weston

Shazor

This is a creative promise ~ my pen will speak to and for the world. Enamored with letters and respectful of their power, I have been writing for most of my life. A mother, daughter, sister and grandmother I give what I have been given, greatfilledly.

Author of . . .

"An Overstanding of an Imperfect Love"

available at Inner Child Press.

www.facebook.com/gailwestonshazor

www.innerchildpress.com/gail-weston-shazor

navypoet1@gmail.com

Homeless Etheree

Bump

Each night

Light wakes me

Shining coldly

Across the car hood

Boy legs are my pillows

Their knees are hurting my head

Mommy says soon we will be home

But she cries over the steering wheel

When she thinks we are already asleep

Retired Double Etheree

She

Used to

Wear diamonds

In her cleavage

Age, her enemy

Marking final battles

In lines around her tight mouth

She bears his happiness with pain

And remembers their wedding story

On the front of society's section

Now even the invitations have stopped

Appearing in her empty mailbox

She could not afford the new dress

He even kept the diamonds

To adorn a new neck

Her young replacement

A new model

A younger

Blonder

She

UnPunked Double Etheree

He

Backs up

Against walls

Cutting his eyes

So hard that he swears

He sees around corners

A valuable talent here

Where the dealers are expecting

He will pay for his junkie mother's

Broken back, last word, spaced out promises

And in the morning when he gets to school

His savings will buy him some heaven

Sunshine and hope in his locker

Just to still his anxious heart

On an empty belly

He sleeps with the iron

Dreaming when he

Might escape

His born

Hell

Albert Infinite Carrasco

Albert Carrasco writes hieroglyphics encrypted in poetic form. His linguistics are not the norm. When it comes to wisdom, sleet ,rain snow and hail its a lyrical storm. He's pure like Fiji, he got the power to hear the dead with no auji. For living a life so tabu, He learnt a die-a-lect , his mouth moves... But at times it's the voice of the crossovers coming through. When he's on stage he has a body temp of 98 degrees... When He recites you feel this chilling breeze, hair stands on skin when he's in the avatar state of his kin. He's non traditional, an unorthodox outspoken urban individual that lived through the subliminal, now he's back to give guidance to his people.

Infinite the poet 2014

Infinite poetry @lulu.com

Alcarrasco2 on YouTube

Infinite the poet on reverbnation

The Poems this month are from my Book

Infinite Poetry

available at

http://www.lulu.com/us/en/shop/al-infinite-carrasco/infinite-poetry/paperback/product-21040240.html

Attempted Suicide

My heart is racing, beating to a drum like a percussionist

Beads of sweat dripping down my body as if I was in shower

These thoughts and voices are far more destructive than peer pressure

They are controlling like a ventriloquist

I'm stuck between a rock and a hard place, life , and a life ending conquest

I have a family that's loves me friends that adore me, but I hate me!

My depression makes me feel I'm less than who I am, a kid full of ambition, to end it all is what I'm wishing.

I've cut at my veins, I popped pills not sooth but to inflict more pain

Why am I alive? I have no idea, these voices say kill myself, so I try. I think its best

So maybe I don't have to live life depressed after death

This will be my third or fourth time in a month I try to succeed in finally finishing

Now its more stitches and stomach flushes after I cut my self and take multiple pills

I Keep trying to take my life, but I don't think its gods will.

How we ate

I would say grace in the street when it was time to eat, lord..." thank you for every thing you do for me. but... my stomach is growling so please guide me through hell in housing, me and my homies are just hungry that's why we're out here living scandalous, some of us are Jehovah's Witness, some Muslim, some Christian. we had religion, its that at certain times our thoughts were blank like atheist living blasphemous for that in god we trust,"... Then we would grab packs out cracks and feed the rush. I didn't want to die. I didn't want my boys to die, but growing up from a boy to a man there was many times I broke down like Wanya because it was so hard to say goodbye to friends of yesterday. I wish that would've stopped me from running the streets. what it did was make me go harder to make ends meet. Although I saw reality I still told myself that can't be me, it was just a matter of time when I would see differently, blam blam slugs tore through me, I got lucky to live, every day I have a reminder in me on how I used to live, when the last blast rung a slug made itself home by my lung, so close, operation wasn't even an option. Still I chose to poverty oppose. I said thanks to the doc and with a cast and cane I was back on the block selling rock cocaine. I was on a relentless run to nowhere, speeding through the ghetto hov lane with no cares, the street was going to have to kill me before I left the game.
It wasn't for fame why I desecrated my last name, it was because I had drive but was driven in the wrong direction. If someone would've taught us a skill other than manufacturing my men probably wouldn't of been dead and i wouldn't have to deal with being a survivor of an attempted assassination. I'm happy that I'm living, just sad that a lot of good men are no longer breathing and can't witness a new beginning... a new found way of eating...expression through writing.

A. lotta kidz

Where I'm from in the ghetto us kids always played rough, we showed each other we were tough. Slap boxing, wrestling, all for one, we played those games as preparation for bully's troublemakers and for those that tap pockets for allowance through intimidation. There was this one boy that never participated and he was a big brawny lad, when the horseplay came his way, with a face of fear he would run away. I used to feel so bad. He was very private, very quiet, none of us really knew anything about him but his name "A. lotta kidz" and that his happy and sad face looked the same...unless he was never happy, but that's impossible, we were kids.

Where ever we went he was always worried about time, I mean really worried. If he had to be home at six he would leave at four thirty to get home early when he was only about fifteen minutes away. He never invited us over, he never offered his phone number, that wasn't a strange thing in the hood because not everyone had a phone and not everybody was okay with company due to bad living conditions shared with their family. When I wanted to hang out with him, I used to whistle downstairs in front of his window, he had asked all of his friends to do so without calling his name, things got stranger.

We met in the winter in the middle of the school year, spring passed and summer came. Its 100 degrees out, all the fellas got together so we can walk to Pelham to jump on the five bus and spend the day at the beach. We all have on summer wear...shorts, sandals and tank tops, not A. Lotta..he wore boots, jeans and a long sleeve shirt, the one thing he has different today than any other day was his shades. They were really dark ones. I remember complimenting him on them and him saying his eyes were sensitive to the bright rays of the sun. We arrive at the beach. Ahhh. What a beautiful day.

We sat on beach chairs and watched all the beautiful girls in bikinis in drooling stares, we're young, to us that's bra and panties. we all had them x rated thoughts when they walked by with a switching strut. I'm looking at A. Lotta actually having a good time. About two hours passed. Everyone is dripping sweat, A. Lotta is dripping wet because he had yet to remove the long sleeve and jeans he wore, nor the shades. One of the fellas gets up and sprints towards the water.. then another and another, soon we are all in the water..except A. lotta. We decide to get out and man handle him in a friendly manner to throw him in. He must've of figured we was coming for him because as we got close he started running. We chased and got him.

We're trying to strip him to his bathing suit, he's putting up a good fight something he never does, through the fun and laughter I noticed he's fighting as if he's fighting for his life. He's not smiling, he's not playing, he was serious, in the moment the fellas didn't notice this. His shades fly off, his shirt gets ripped off, his jeans get lowered but he doesn't have a bathing suit, he has boxers on. His eyes are black, he has lacerations all over his back, his legs are bruised his arms have burn marks and scabs on top of new scars cause old wounds haven't heeled. I grabbed him and asked who did this, crying in fear and shame he mumbles... this is why I couldn't give you my number or invite y'all over, it was forbidden by my abusive father. This is A. lotta kidz story.... A lot of kids.

Siddartha

Beth

Pierce

Siddartha Beth Pierce is a Mother, Poet, Artist and African and Contemporary Art Historian. Her art, poetry and teaching were featured on PBS in April 2001 while she was the Artist-in-Residence and Associate Professor at Virginia State University in Petersburg, Virginia. She received her BA in Studio Art from George Mason University in Fairfax, Virginia and her M.A.E. from Virginia Commonwealth University in Richmond, Virginia. She continued into PhD. Studies in African and Contemporary Art studies at Virginia Commonwealth University where she is now All but Dissertation. Her works of poetry and art have been featured in numerous newspaper articles, journals, magazines and chapbooks.

http://www.innerchildpress.com/siddartha-beth-pierce.php

http://www.youtube.com/watch?v=OQ87NrLt_to

http://www.writerscafe.org/Siddartha

No More Wire Hangers

Fluorescent
lights
Balding
Rays.

Blinded
afflicted
Flattened
Bed of nails
She laid
Awake
aware
stiff, taut.

Her daughter,
Eden
The womb, the angel
Petrified
vacuumed
suctioned
Slurped
agony
Cocooned
and Lost.

The Bloody Corpse
traipsed
away
upon the flat iron death bed
flushed for vegetation.

The teenager
remained
medicated
for several
hours
in a daze
and spoke
not a
word
of the
Matter.

Sirens

The attack-
the attic nap yarded
quilted
As the sitter sat before
soap operas
Her son stole away
to the loft
molested the four year old girl
where the sun don't shine.

He warned-
'I will kill your parents
if you ever tell that I have touched you'

She told eventually
they reported next door
and the old woman cried
for his curiosity-

Fire department volunteer
was he-
and to this day
when the red truck
blows by
alarming the neighborhoods
she secretly wishes
that he would die
in a pyre of those flames.

The attack-
the attic nap yarded
quilted
As the sitter sat before
soap operas
Her son stole away
to the loft
molested the four year old girl
where the sun don't shine.

He warned-
'I will kill your parents
if you ever tell that I have touched you'

She told eventually
they reported next door
and the old woman cried
for his curiosity-

Fire department volunteer
was he-
and to this day
when the red truck
blows by
alarming the neighborhoods
she secretly wishes
that he would die
in a pyre of those flames.

Her Voice

The young girl lay upon the ground
spread-eagled
on a dark, deserted road
waiting to be found
as from the distance a Light
approached.

She could not make out a face
but heard the words
'The Truth you seek is your Voice.'

She arose having found the answer
she sought
as she brushed off her dirty knees determinedly
she did not see or hear the oncoming semi
sweep her off her feet once again.

She lay upon the ground
spread-eagled
on a dark, deserted road
waiting to be found
as from the distance a Light
approached
enveloping her wholly
consumed by the Light
her voice became one of the millions
that had crossed this road before
falling sweetly, knowingly upon death's door
to be heard from nevermore.

Janet
Perkins
Caldwell

Janet wrote her first poems and short stories in an old diary where she noted her daily thoughts. She wrote whether suffering, joyful or hoping for peace in the world. She started this process at the tender age of Eight. This was long before journaling was in vogue.

Along with her thoughts, poetry and stories, she drew what she refers to as Hippie flowers. Janet still to this day embraces the Sixties and Seventies flower power symbol, of peace and love, which are a very important part of her consciousness.

Janet wrote her first book, in those unassuming diaries, never to be seen by the light of day due to an unfortunate house fire. This did not deter her drive. She then opted for a new batch of composition journals and filled everyone. In the early nineteen-eighties, Janet held a byline in a small newspaper in Denton, Texas while working full time, being a Mother and attending Night School.

Since the early days Janet has been published in newspapers, magazines and books globally. She also has enjoyed being the feature on numerous occasions, both in Magazines, Radio and on a plethora of Sites. She has gone on to publish three books. *5 degrees to separation* 2003, *Passages* 2012 and her latest book *Dancing Toward the Light . . . the journey continues* 2013. All of her Books are available through Inner Child Press along with Fine Book Stores Globally. Janet P. Caldwell is also the Chief Operating Officer of Inner Child ltd.

http://www.janetcaldwell.com/

http://www.innerchildpress.com/janet-p-caldwell.php

https://www.facebook.com/JanetPCaldwell

5 degrees to separation

I learned to count early
Read the bible too
Wrath, punishment
Seemed no absolution
Separate at five

In the morning
When I was defiled
Five screams a minute
Five shiny points from
The glass shards

Five fingers, to check off
As I calculate
In five minutes I'm clean
and new
Separated by five degrees

Five from what I don't want
To remember, anything green
Black or brown

Make it easier
Five letters/numbers are my friends

The ceiling fan;
Wood, glass, white, brown, brass
Another set of quints
A quick escape
When I should need one
My rabbit hole with
Back-doors aplenty
Five senses all shut down
I've got good and can count
Before what might happen.

Safe in numbers, hidden
When I separate from myself.

Weep For the Child That Never Was

Tears fall down my face
for a child with no name
A child filled with anguish
suffering disgrace

How could they have lied
and treated her so
Why didn't they love her
just let her go?

Buy her new clothes
fill her with song
Mess her up more
you can't be wrong!

She grew up with walls
forever all around
The music you played
she couldn't hear a sound

You look at her now
with disgust in your eyes
You can't see her though
she wears a disguise

Hand-made by you
so carefully sewn
With coagulated drops
all her own

You thought that you knew her
but there's no way that you could
She's not what you think
behind the mask stained with blood

Daddy # 2

I Remember (him)
Glassy blue eyes
Fingertips brown
Black greasy hair
Forehead high
Child killer
Sick bastard

I Remember (me)
Scuttling like a rat
Running from a cat
Scattering across the tile
Like a roach on fire
When the lights came on
Better scatter, Daddy's home!

I Remember (séances)
Straddling his head
The shoulders so high
Calling up the dead
Peering in the sky
Let the dead now arise
It'll stop daddy's cries

I Remember (abuse)
Dancing to the belt
That beat me blue
Decorated with welts
Daddy, I remember you . . .

June 'Bugg' Barefield

June Barefield ~ Poet-Activist-Teacher-Author

Born and raised in the Midwest, currently residing in East St Louis, IL. Junes interests include long walks, sunrises, cheesecake, and words. He considers the NRA, and it's supporters 2B a 21st century Nazi-ism! The author of two collections of poetry which include B4 the Dawn, and The Journeyman

I B. Self educated, and proud to be humbled. An avid reader, and teacher, counselor in his community at what we as a society have termed "at risk children". June refers to them as Gang members, and dope dealers. A brilliant speaker, and motivator; fluent in at least three religions! June's favorite quote: "FUCK THE SYSTEM!"

for booking call : 720 404 8563

http://authorsdb.com/authors-directory/2292-june-barefield

you can get more of June here . . .

https://www.facebook.com/JuneBugg900

https://www.facebook.com/june.barefield.7

http://www.innerchildpress.com/june-barefield.php

"BIG HOMIE SAY"

"Where to go, what to do?"
"I'll pursue this life of crime; so fuck a job
and fuck school too!"
"I'm never taking what they offering fool.
"And how long will this last? "My entire community
is on dope, taking them good, l00000NG blasts..."
"It ain't no money in that though; I'll end up stealing
from my mother..."
"So, instead I'm like my brother's keeper; Got these
Nigga's out here going to see the Grim Reaper!"
My BIG HOMIE SAY...

"You can't wait for the next man to give you shit!"
"Can't switch it up; Gotta be down to RYDE 4 the click!"
He said, "The enemy rolled up on him today bustin', but
them damn fools missed..."
BIG HOMIE SAY...

He said, "He copped my first case ate thee age of ONE-
THREE."
Said, "He beat a bitch so bad that now he has bad
dreams..."
BIG HOMIE SAY...

"The right to remain silent is a mutha fuckin' joke."
He passed me the blunt,
I thought about it for a sec
Took me one of them little bitty ass tokes, you know?
I thought a little more, and then I took my young ass
home!!

Tell Them

Tell them that after they have learned to read
to write
fumBle about with their computers
B not distracted
there's more to learn to bring forth
solutions
tell them that they R being educated just to conduct the
nations LABOR
and while they R told they R free
tell them to oBserve they're own family
Still slaves
2 the dollar bill
tell em learn the dynamic of economics
the tricks unlearned
4 the treats being served
across the traks
out of sight sound or touch
of the INNER city
where ALL lines R
BLURRED.
Tell them
the TRUFF.

A VERSE.

My bedroom used to B so dark I thought I'd become an astronaut
There was a ferocious crocodile behind my closet door
I'd lock him inside & hide; afraid of the shifting shadows on the wall, the hollering in the hall; I felt so small
Time and again I would crawl into myself, and imagine I was somewhere else
Never screamed out once, but
I wanted help...
I found my comfort outdoors running & jumping
Playing in the streets
At home my mother preached
ducking left hooks, and throwing books in a corrupted flux of "fuck you's" & "I don't give a fucks"
Waiting 4 someone to come in and kiss me goodnight
Knowing damn well they had to first finish the fight
Heart beating like the meanest kid on the playground now, and
Made me want to break something.

I'd like to maybe sniff the glue that binds families together
Get some attention before I reach detention
B the smart kid just once, and revel in my clever
Never did sit on daddy's lap
Most of the words he had for me tasted a lot like uncooked carp
To me, he was always a fishy ni99a
It would take a little time, but soon enough I'd imitate the fool and steal all his fuckin' liquor
Every now and then my momma would swing me in her arms like a chandelier, and that was nice
but fleeting...
Mostly though, to be precise
I only wanted 2 break something

Debbie

M.

Allen

Debbie M. Allen is a Pennsylvania native that has remained true to her passion for the love of poetry. She has always had a passion for poetry. In 2010 she took that passion and made it her cause, always maintaining the truth of her experiences and the beliefs she holds dear.

Debbie is the Author of "A Poet Never Dies," her first book of poetry which was published in 2012. Since then she has published her second book of poems, "The Spiral of a Pisces: In Manic Flow," which encompasses her ever spiraling transition of expression. She can be found participating in various avenues of spoken word and poetry under the pseudonym D. Flo'essence including The Truth Commission Movement, Penology Ink Productions, Jersey Radical Productions and What's The News.

Shelter Note

Child...

Things are bound to get easier

Even when the toddle of tales are gone...

And the flatter of new fawn wears off your skin...

As long as you remember

Never let your reflection dull

In dirty mirrors...

I know it's like hear say in a court of

Passing years

Yet judgment only passes

Into weakened ears...

If you let the echo of despair

Bounce too hard against your ear drums

Suffocating your beat

Into a conundrum of stutters

In the hurt of aching feet...

Youth grow out of shoes so quickly

But we can always walk in the stellar of faith...

Bypassing the hateful lacing of reality

That seems to trip every step

Before you get to see traces of that yellow brick road...

Time gets as old as re-runs of life episodes
But the heart is an abode of new themes
Hold your esteem like gold to shield from its breaking
Making yourself a star
That shines even when the sun
Can't divide clouded lines...
Shake your senses beyond the crime
Of groundless thinking
Settle yourself in the battle against shrinking...
Because...child...
Things are bound to get easier
As long as tall is how you stand in
Sheltered notes to self
Knowing that if you ever need help
There are hands always ready to lift you...
Those footprints in the sand
Never disappear...

Unknown Daughter

I feel like I was hated since the day I was born…
Uterine scorn
How I can I live in that shadow?
Daddy was a pan handler of panties
And mama handed choices over
In the bottom of his bucket…
So my birth didn't fit their budget
I became a woman from lessons of a woman darned
Of ragged yarn…
And daddy was a word I only uttered
In soul poems…
Who are you? So I can know me…
But that would never be
Because he was just a figment in the mind of prisons…
Society given
Never being more than the word of a senseless man
Because actions don't know sense
In hollow glands…
So he never sweated me…daddy…
And mommy…
I was a lil shoulder for her heavy tears to cry on…
Killing my years too early
Surely if I had been a seed…she would have grown me…
If seeds could grow from ill thought dreams
From killed out schemes that had her reeling…
So my hands are constantly dealing
Worn out Aces…that never traced back to one…
I am just the chip in argued fits of lackluster worth
Bursting at the seams …
With no stitch to at least trick me into believing
I would be whole again…

Mommy and daddy….
They call me their twin…
Does that mean I will meet the same unconscious end?
That they met….
Sometimes I regret being born…
But that is not really my regret to hold…
I just held the coffin of a womb
Under bitterness boldness…for a moment…
Used to carry the load of their weakness…
There is no real deepness in that
Just shallow snaps of a cord that never
Would lead back to life…
No hype…no future in fairness
Only careless hugs that left me colder than
The slap of the doctor's hand that gave me first
Sting of reality…
I was never meant to be
Special…
I was always the special of the day
Thigh claps on the lap
Of worthlessness…
Mommy and daddy lost my hope in craps
That morning…
Dawning me into another generation of misery…
And yes…I will remember
How they cheated me…
In raptures seemingly
Only rupturing me
In the claims or an unknown daughter…

The Sovereignty of My Verses

Childhood was a bitter beast
Battling loneliness that seemed to
Bagger me into sleep…
Bullied by nightmares…because
Nobody cares to dream about lost children
So I became misplaced…vanishing
Slowly until there was no trace
Of adolescence…
Arthritic in my thoughts…
Caught up in magnitudes small hands could never grasp
Until tiny fingers gave clasp

Around the barrel of a pen…

Ink and I became very best friends
Playing patty-cake around verses
In make believe universes that saved me
From being alone…
And gave words the perfect home to live in…
Strengthening a broken spirit
Baring a gift that made Christmas year round
Although it wasn't Santa but God that gave me my poetic crown
Knowing Princesses still have fears to live in…

And Lord knows
Teenage years split hairs to no end…
Body begat a womb
That the lust of men tried to fit in…
Spreading the seed that spread legs to urgency
I…believing time developed my hour glass shape

To curve along the raping of my fate…
The girl six of their fantasy birthing wisdom too late
Mommy became my name before
Creation could create a woman…
So the mimic of grown hands

Sought a childhood friend in my pen

Trying to fit mothering in a world
Where mothering was a metaphor run thin?
Searching for anything to bring shame understanding…
Hands shaky in the skipping of ages
Until rings on a spiral notebook became the engagement
Of pages…
Writing hope into my youth
And as my belly grew
So did the space of my expression…
Keeping me divided from despair
With lessons scrolled in stages of quills giving self
A selfless muse to be still in…
Baby birthing baby
Streamed in black rivers of my ink…
Cradling her with kisses of the messages
That kept my heart in sync at the beating of her bay…
Lines leading to the future
Defined by the hymns I bore her…
Humming peace in the ripple of poetry to unknown waters

Then the years cursed breaths in the drown of torture…
Smacked into me with the death of hands
Demanding that my life only live along the bank of
Of caging borders…
Two daughters, two sons and me with
Broken love that broke the run of my words…

Mocking birds singing tone deaf
To the disorder of my verbs…
Wing clipped prayers unable to filter tales
To the expiration of my soul…
Decomposed…unheard…
While I pondered the scripture of headstones
Hurled at the hellish spin of destiny
Trying to best me out of what I once found
In my own sacred terms
Yet memories stole away in the back of my mind
Reminded me that words never burn…

In the ashes of defeat
Laid my pen rendered steel
Welded over time to remain the one thing real
I could feel…clutched deep inside
Turning water wheels to purge me of my cries…
So I can will a bit of heaven
Gold lined sheets I now walk in the paving of my rhyme
Influenced divine…everlasting beyond the caving of life
A sanctuary within

My survival story
Through the power of my pen…

Tony Henninger

Tony Henninger

Tony has been writing for about 20 years. He has published one book titled " A Journey of Love." He has also contributed to several Anthologies. His book is available at Innnerchild Press and Amazon.com.

You can find him at Facebook.com/Tony Henninger

Linkdin.com/Tony Henninger or

tonyhenninger@yahoo.com

Remember

Do you remember being a child?
When the skies were bluest blue
and the future looked so bright?
Everything was possible then.
Imagination was unbound.

Pretending to fly so high,
soaring up, down, and around,
like the birds in the sky.
Then falling to the ground
with belly aching laughter.

What a beautiful sight,
children at play in the meadow.
Twirling around with delight.
Chasing their own shadows.
Searching for the end of the rainbow.

Remember those treasured times
and help stamp out the crimes
committed on children today,
both, near and far away.

We must cherish and nurture
the life of a child.

Our future depends on it….

A Child's Smile

On a beautiful, sunny afternoon
I was sitting on a park bench
enjoying the serenity and beauty
of watching children at play,
thinking ,"Ah, what a rare sight today."
Unbound, unafraid, imaginations soaring.
Lost in their own little world, not knowing,
just a few feet away, the real world
stood cold and foreboding.
Can you hear the cries in the night?
Of loneliness, hunger, and fright?
Places where there are no parks.
Where there are no children at play.
Where children are "things" owned.
Burdens, mistakes, or baggage,
and sometimes even garbage
to be used and thrown away.
In these, so-called, "civilized days"
it is appalling and sad to see
a child not able to be a child
yet, still giving love unconditionally.

Love lies in a child's smile,
not in the tears on their face.

Bring out their wondrous smile
and this world will be a better place

for all.

A Mistake

On a cold dark night
misty from the rain,
far away from the light
near an old storm drain,

She lay crying.

Unheard and unwanted,
freezing to her bones,
pleading for the warmth
that left her on the cold stones,

She lay sighing.

All alone and full of fright,
reaching out for a love token,
as under darkness of the night
a mother/child bond was broken,

She lay dying.

Tossed aside….

A Mistake….

Joe
Da Verbal
MindDancer

Joseph L Paire' aka Joe DaVerbal Minddancer . . . is a quiet man, born in a time where civil liberties were a walk on thin ice. He's been a victim of his own shyness often sidelined in his own quest for love. He became the observer, charting life's path. Taking note of the why, people do what they do. His writings oft times strike a cord with the dormant strings of the reader. His pen the rosined bow drawn across the mind. He comes full-frontal or in the subtlest way, always expressing in a way that stimulate the senses.

https://www.facebook.com/joe.minddancer

Letter To Daddy

The water falls over my body as hot as I can stand it.
I scrub and scrub to the point my skin is raw.
The full bar of soap I started with has withered to a sliver
In my hand, I hold a loofah its pores filled with my pain.
I feel stained in shame; it will not wash down the drain.
Daddy I feel I am to blame; it is insane
However, my brain tells me I am dirty.

I can't run to you and say Daddy he hurt me.
You're off fighting a war see! Mama won't hear me
It's her lover that…OH GOD PLEASE.
Let this soap wash away from me this terrible memory.
How could she take from me, my private sanctity?
Just to satisfy his lust for me,
My own Mother has no love for me.

DADDY; Please come home to me
Maybe you can set me free.
I can't regain my dignity, will I become a whore like she?
I pray and bath constantly to remove their sins off of me
I'm being used and abused repeatedly.
I know this hurts you to read Daddy, it's killing me.

I am trying hard Daddy, but no one will listen
Every time I go outside people are whispering
The boys think I am easy, the girls call me fast.
Mama and he are drinking now, DADDY
I don't know how much longer I can last.

Listen To Them

Red and Blue flashing lights; Clear Clear.
We almost lost her.
Poor little thing she's so beautiful
Hang on lovely one; we are almost here.
Come-on Doc; please; you've got to save her
Pulse is weak; Lord God my Savior..
See the light see the shadow going up or down below.
It's judgment time; for this life she tried to take..
Caught up in life; caught up in turmoil's wake
Dealing with loneliness;   surrounded by crowds
Which one among you;
Now wipe the sweat off your brow.

Fun on the outside crying with-in
She talked to her mother; she is not listening
Family woes, family throws as many hard punches
As the ones, we do not know.
Be hard be strong be like the rest
Will this behavior help pass life's test?
Dealing with school dealing with fools
Dealing with Moms perverted friends;
She cannot prove

Alone in a world all about self, no structure is the culture
It's all about wealth; Get money get ends make that paper
Your friend just raped her; now she tries to escape her!
You can't be found; because you're on your own caper
Look at the shadows, which one is next
The oldest the youngest; the in between
Any family any where life shattered dreams

When a loved one cries out; is it get back in the race?
Or taking time out to hear out the case
Flat line_______________ she did not make it,
She took the life she felt was forsaken
Her Mother thought her lover; she had taken
Wouldn't hear she had been raped then
Cause of death Suicide...
Hidden facts for "Family Pride"
Heaven's door, was opened wide
Listen to Them ...All Kids Don't Lie..........Peace

Hand Me Down

Hey, man is you all right.
Looks like you got the worst of that fight.
It had to be more than three;
You're twice as big as me.

Girl, did that fool hit you again?
Oh my god girl look at your eye
I told you them boy's ain't bout nothing.
All they want is a little humping

Yeah man they got me good,
Yeah girl he was tripping.
Both of them embarrassed
To say they got whippings

Daddy drinks too much
Mama on some otherworld tip
The both of them;
From pasts that tolerated it.

Spare the rod; spoil the child
Moms too afraid when Dad gets wild
3, 5, 7 year old boys punched like men
2, 4, 6 year old girls looked upon as women.

Ghetto life, Suburban living
Rural communities or Backwoods' hillbillies
Some parent or relative are slapping them silly.
He fell down the stairs, She's on her monthlies

Notes to schools when they don't show up promptly
Explanations when the cops come on your property.
Scared children lie in the hopes they'll find peace.
Instead it's see what you did, you caused me misery.

And the hands come down again and again.
It never ends; Siblings cower and wonder whose next
Sometimes it's the youngest, sometimes the eldest
They walk on eggshells at home, it's very complex.

Baby girl grows breast, the oldest tries to teach her
Tape them down, it's for the best, yes it's a mess.
There is very little intervention, the authorities try
But it's hard to pay attention.

So many fall through the cracks
Mostly it's a case of too late.
Those that make it from under, carry a heavy weight.

Failed relationships; marriages and such.
Some carry over that same mentality
Held in by that crust; Open your eyes.

Better yet open your mouths
Seeing a child beat down, is not entertainment.
"None of your business"
Will you say that at the arraignment?

How we are taught right from wrong
Does make a difference.
How some of us; were taught!
Has made; some of us oblivious.

Hand down some knowledge
Hand down some land
Hand down some love.
Just handing down hands.

Robert Gibbons

Robert Gibbons

Robert Gibbons moved to New York City in the summer of 2007 in search of his muse-Langston Hughes. Robert has performed all over New York City.

His first collection of Poetry, Close to the Tree was published by Threes Rooms Press and can be purchased at :

www.threeroomspress.com

You may contact Robert
via his FaceBook presences :

www.facebook.com/anthonyrobertgibbons

www.facebook.com/jamesmercerlangstonhughes

for the young and modern Martin Luther King

"why should the world be otherwise, in counting all our tears and sighs?"
(after Paul Laurence Dunbar)

Avonte Oquendo

your story is my story
one with horror and expectation
walking out of school for the last
time is always the issue
the underground of subways
and transient byways
and autistic sounds
garbles the thousands
hallucinations, our nursery
of fears and bedlam of
emotion finding bones
near the Harlem river
the baptism of Emmet Till
kingdom come

Patrick Alford

I saw a police
in the twisting streets of Brooklyn
this is made for television
for those that think
it is real but it is and they
forget he is still missing
with your broken amber alerts
and milk carton face
who am I to judge
when they take out the trash
and through his humanity
down the chute

Trayvon Martin

you were not old
enough to dream just
an explosion of manliness
in a childhood frame
and you had no choice
your shroud incriminates
and the loud body parts

are massive but you were built
for war and the sniper
takes aim
and won

Kevin Miller

and momma greatest fear
is to send her child out
before dark, I can imagine
a kitchen table with
a space
empty

Myls Dobson

and Jesus claims the body
hanging like a tortured phrase
and the wages of sin
is death, and the grave
marker shall read
baby

seven blocks home

(for Leiby Kletzky, 8)

it takes compassion to navigate the crooked streets of
Brooklyn
each block has it own personality, its own nationality; its
own
language, its own persuasion; there are seven blocks and
seven
days and seven complete revolutions; seven demarcations
seven solution and seven times seven is seemingly
historic in proportion, there are countless children hiding
in the subways of New York and D. C. and Oakland seven
missing expired milk cartons from the lunch room
refrigerator
seven amber alerts and photographs unseen unheard unfelt
unknown in this death notebook the same cry comes from
my
Yiddish tongue from this elegy in song; it is a lamentation
this seven is orthodoxy; it is democracy because the world
is so small seven can chant like a cantor; we cant call it
evil
because our only focus is God.

the ban on saggy pants

I do not always agree with you, as a child I was rebellious
did not understand my hormones; my mother said it was
the mark of my father; the toddler of his double; but
somehow I was saved; the mazes of childhood and puberty
the elmer's glue of family; we had belts and buckles around
our house; Easter suits and baggy pants; but then there
was the style; could never grow an afro; my hair just
would not develop; so had to envelope a lesser do, the few
of us remain without high top and fade; without box cut
or the name inscribed on the side of our skull; the lull
to be popular; the rock stars of high school

do not always agree with you; the boys on the corner
could stay out later; could hang until the street lights
would darken; would look at them from my window
would wish I could be like them; but my parents were
insistent; they had a plan for me; they demanded of me
to be individual; not a gang; or a group; or a fade
but home made; they way each day to say grace
or do not forget to say thank you; I did not always
agree, but I am a free from the judgment of others

the push and pull of peer pressure; create my own
sense; lenses of wisdom from a mother's tongue
the few among that can not develop into their own
the sad song of living this way; the price of another
elegy; beg them to be free; in some way this is what
the metaphor means; their way of trying to be free
beg them to be free; release them from restriction
their pants are just back drops; beg them to be free
knocking down of walls; as tall as inhibition; listen
to what they wants as they walk down these roads
of forgetfulness; the instinct of toughness; beg them
to be free; then maybe there will be some that will
understand the band; and sanction; the pent -up
and the anxious; really they are not free; just look
and then you will see.

Neetu
Wali

Neetu Wali

Hi! I am Neetu. Who am I? This question is very difficult to answer.

Well! If you insist, let me reveal. I am a human and like every other human I eat, sleep, drink, dance, sing, laugh, smile, cry and so on. Hang on! There is a difference. Unlike most of the human beings, I breathe and when I breathe, I relax. When I am relaxed, I draw. I draw sketches of me in words.

I have been orbiting around sun for forty years now. I started this journey on the Valentine day of 1974. I have seen people craving for heaven and I was born in the only heaven on earth (Kashmir). My Grandfather was a spiritual personality and a renowned poet of his time. Though he left me around 35 years ago, I couldn't let him go. I carry him in my eyes and mind and will do that till the end of my life. I hate words, yet I am full of words. I know words cannot express, yet I express me through words, because they are the only medium I am familiar with. That is why I try to express me as much as possible with as minimum words as possible.

When I did Masters in business administration, I never knew, writing will be the only business in my life. More than hobby writing is a necessity for me, because it helps me get the load of thoughts off my head. I don't remember when it that I wrote my first poem was. But I surely know the time of my last poem. Surely, not before my last breath.

Skirt in Dirt

Dirty eyes around her
Played with her torn skirt
While she played with dirt
She did play with dirt
But she didn't know
What it meant to play
With dirt
Till she actually
Was forced to be the
Dirt to play with
She lived
A death inside
And how that mattered
To the world outside
The world needed
Her skin
Not the soul within
And now something
Inside her says
Time for another skirt
Another round of dirt
And she asks herself
Should I??

Cage of Age

Wrinkled face
Age sprinkled everywhere
Like colours wide and vast
Yet so colourless
Eyes emotionless
Yet oceans of emotions
Hidden within
Life so intense
Beyond experience
Nothing else
Just life
Pure life
Moments count and add
One by one
As breath revives
A moment of life survives
With no clue
Of how and why
Just life
Pure life
Please never ask

When you see
A hand that is
Soft bones covered with hard skin
Holding abnormally tight
And stoic eyes
Staring innocently wild
A platter full
Coz it is neither taste
Nor texture
Just life
Ounces of pure life
Life signs a secret lease
Always keen to release
This is just
A cute try to trap a cage
Cage of age

Train of Thoughts

Train of thoughts
Run across the brain
A thought gets down
And a new one boards
The roads never end
Thoughts are never dead
Without any brakes
The train runs amuck
Brake-less and driver-less
End of this journey
Is the end of life
And the goal of journey
Becomes the goal of life
We all are placed
Where our thoughts place us
A deed is done
First in thought
An achievement is achieved
First in thought
A crime is committed
First in thought
A sin happens
First in thought
A life comes free
When a thought is brought

Shareef

Abdur

Rasheed

Shareef Abdur-Rasheed,AKA,Zakir Flo was born and raised in Brooklyn, New York. His education includes Brooklyn College, Suffolk County Community College and Makkah, Saudi Arabia. He is a Veteran of the Viet Nam era, where in 1969 he reverted to his now reverently embraced Islamic Faith. He is very active in the Islamic community and beyond with his teachings, activism and his humanity.

Shareef's spiritual expression comes through the persona of "Zakir Flo" . Zakir is Arabic for "To remind". Never silent, Shareef Abdur-Rasheed is always dropping science, love, consciousness and signs of the time in rhyme.

Shareef is the Patriarch of the Abdur-Rasheed Family with 9 Children (6 Sons and 3 Daughters) and 42 Grandchildren (24 Boys and 18 Girls).

For more information about Shareef,
contact or follow him at :

http://www.facebook.com/shareef.abdurrasheed1

http://zakirflo.wordpress.com/

http://www.innerchildpress.com/shareef-abdur-rasheed.php

https://www.facebook.com/pages/Muslim-Writers-Forum/370511683056503

sullen..,

faces looking in space
these reps of the humanrace
cross eachother's paths
everyday never so much
as a word to say
do they look into anothers
eyes..,
try to visualize how is their
lives?
how do they live,for what do
they live?
how much of a dam do we give
call it live 'n' let live?
how many years did you ride by
their side
look into space,blank look in their
eyes?

going to and from where ever their
going to ,coming from
age of technology has digressed
from humanity
and they call this progress,civilized
or is this insanity collectively
conceptualized
can we make a change,a difference
or remain a society of indifference
institutionalized
untill our demise is realized?
how can we grow and thrive
when humans perpetually show
little or no humanity
riding side by side?

in real time!

gestures to restore order
tend to border on the
absurd
considering the masses
kicked to the curb,
literally!
left to rot like corpses
labeled collateral damage
by the world's governments
controlled by their corporate
bosses!
scorned,ignored,lives torn
drivin from their homes
in droves
left to wander the roads
with what possessions they
were able to load!
posturing,rethoric,sound bites
is by far the relief sent to the
millions of wretched souls in
flight
who everyday have to fight to
to have the right to stay on this
cold earth another day!

who can feel the refugee
driven away from their homes
with families to roam?

yet we can sit safely
with the audacity to complain
about what amounts to bull$h!t
by name
compared to those who's lives
were delt serious blows
enduring human suffering that
most will never know!
as it's intended insolation shows
once again the people have been
abandoned,offended!
and will continue to provided
mankind stays divided as intended!

food 4 thought!

born of..,

the forlorn, abandoned scorned,
hidden in full sight
the plight of those the system
oppose and constantly deprive
of rights

born of..,

the forlorn, abandoned, scorned

from day one was branded
told to hold the hand it was
handed from a marked deck
holding jokers smirking @ ya
in disrespect!
you lose! what you expect
life can be a bitch!
born naked, die barefoot
with no shoes, not even a
stitch!
born to lose from da roots
how you gonna "Pull yourself
up by your bootstraps"
when you ain't got no boots!
answer..,
you still have the means
to "choose" life and fight!
go from upside down
to upright!
refuse to accept the brand
stand up and take a stand

faith, honesty, consistency
hard work, dependability,
humility,
can translate into legitimate
viability!
put an end to self denial
accepting labels vile
all da while of course
force a fake smile!
tap dance 'n' grin
while inside you hate the
the skin your in
it's a dam sin, no way to
live
born to die forlorned, scorned
like you never was here, or
ever been!
dam shame because you caved,
gave in,. never tried to rise!!
bad way to live, worst way to die!

food 4 thought!

Kimberly Burnham

An Integrative Medicine practitioner, Kimberly Burnham uses poetry, words, coaching and hands-on therapies to help you heal. A published poet in several Inner Child Press anthologies, including Healing Through Words and I Want My Poetry To, Kimberly is winner of SageUSA's story contest with a poem about her 2013 Hazon CrossUSA bicycle ride. She is writing The Journey Home about that 3000 mile expedition.

Now, you get to be her muse with a list of seven experiences you yearn for. She writes a poem as if already, you are feeling the exhilaration of living your dreams.

You can find Kimberly ...

http://www.KimberlyBurnhamPhD.com

http://www.linkedin.com/in/KimberlyBurnham

http://www.amazon.com/Kimberly-Burnham/e/B0054RZ4A0

Let The Child Write a Poem

Whether a small child
using words
expressing big feelings
or an inner child
grown wise
through experiences
histories portraying
hope
so different
from your own

Help her see
the world
through a new lens
shapes shift
yet stable enough
to walk forward
learning to balance
unique differences

Shine a light
a softer touch
for him
all feelings welcome
finding ways to channel
energy and emotions
like a river bed
into a broad field
nourishing carrots

Words raining down
on children
you choose the effect
the path to the heart
impacts on
time
space
me

Are You A Child's Mirror

Imagine everyone
around a mirror
reflecting back
who you are
you think
it's accurate
a steady clear mirror
instead like a funhouse glass
tall and wavy
short and blurry
who you are
reflected back

Words spoken in anger
in haste
defining your potential
seem to reflect reality
only of those
who unaware
look not through
the reflection
to the inner core
more precious than diamonds
shaped with skill
or crushed by blood

Opposites Attract

Parents so different
in this world of duality
don't make me choose
who is right
who is wrong
teach me
difference is good

I am unique
that makes me
wonderful
trying to conform
I see conformity's benefits
but I am different
I can change
not enough
to meet
a world of expectations

I hear the drum
tapping in my head
as present in my body
I sway back and forth
my heart expands
my mind quiets
and I witness myself
reflecting outward in joy

William

S.

Peters, Sr.

Bill's writing career spans a period quickly approaching 50 years. Being first Published in 1972, Bill has since went on to Author 24 additional Volumes of Poetry, Short Stories, etc., expressing his thoughts on matters of the Heart, Spirit, Consciousness and Humanity. His primary focus is that of Love, Peace and Understanding!

Bill is the Founding Director of Inner Child Enterprises as well as the Past Director of Publicity for Society Hill Music.

Bill says . . .
I have always likened Life to that of a Garden. So, for me, Life is simply about the Seeds we Sow and Nourish. All things we "Think and Do", will "Be" Cause and eventually manifest itself to being an "Effect" within our own personal "Existences" and "Experiences" . . . whether it be Fruit, Flowers, Weeds or Barren Landscapes! Bill highly regards the Fruits of his Labor and wishes that everyone would thus go on to plant "Lovely" Seeds on "Good Ground" in their own Gardens of Life!

to connect with Bill, he is all things Inner Child :
www.iaminnerchild.com

Personal Web Site
www.iamjustbill.com

help

she cried all night

every night

and i could not understand it

i was loosing my tolerance

and i realized

we both needed help

Alone

yes she had thoughts
of what she wanted to be
and they were beginning to come together
in how she saw her self

she knew nothing of
Sleeping Beauty
though she was one of her own

she dreamed of such personages as
Nicki Minaj, Lindsay Lohan
and the Kardashian Girls
that's what she wanted to be
another Robyn "Ri Ri" Rihanna
or a Beyonce
so she could live the life
she was being taught should be

but it was all beyond her

all she knew
was she did not want to be
like her Mom
alone

Help Lizzy

the Cabs were busy
and there was a girl named Lizzy
looking for a free ride
walking the streets
looking for treats
for her best friend, her mother had died

she was lost and alone
a runaway from home
and a Father she never knew
she did not understand
just what was God's plan
neither do i, do you ?

she had lost all her hope
she was now doing dope
doing tricks to feed her vice
sometimes she would cry
and just wish she could die
yet she bore her cross like Christ

she was only fourteen
with no shoulder to lean
no Mother nor Father nor Friend
if you should see her about
be a caring soul and reach out
and bring Lizzy's story to an end.

May Features

~ * ~

Joski the Poet

ReeCee

Shannon Stanton

Joski
The Poet

Joski The Poet

Joski The Poet has appeared live at several venues all around as well various competitions such as : Battle of the Sexes, The Men of Erotic and also poetry for Cancer project. You can also find me as a regular supporter and contributor of different online shows as well.

Through Joski The Poet's eyes Poetry for me is and always has been, one of the most beautiful art forms around. Whether I'm writing a strong socially conscious piece I feel the need more to let the light shine on through poetry or to reach the hearts and souls of those who read my work and support me. Every type of poetry has it's place in any poetry community.

I initially was introduced to poetry through my best friend Tonya Moore who is wonderful Poetess in her own right. I was told about a website called GS Poetry. I was intrigued. I began writing short erotic stories and would then email them to friends to share. Soon after my short stories caught the attention of a few people affiliated with various magazines who soon inquired if I would be able to write short stories and also turn my short stories into poems. I later branched over to Face book to expand my ink game there and network with fellow Poets.

I also have a music background and love to sing when time and circumstances allow. Poetic Influences In my opinion all poetry is beautiful and should be read simply because it is an expression. Some of my early poetry influences are : Maya Angelou, Marcus, Garvey, Rakim & 2pac. Other influences include : King David from the Bible. I find his words to be melodic.

Joski The Poet's Vision

My vision for poetry is no matter what form you choose. Make sure you're doing it for the love of the art!

twisted sister

She wore decorated tears to protect her
Painted pain on her face by the men who would molest her
Undress her
Right under her mother's nose
Mother did not notice she woke up in her other clothes
I regret this image I must project
about this fragile little doll in the projects
Her mom failed this frail object,
As his torture he subjects
Never would she view her man as a suspect
or
Suspect that he would have sex
With her baby
she would whisper through her tears, "God save me"
Lately her next future ex
Paid midnight visits
No need to knock on her door for she knew who is it
He would lie in her baby's secret garden
He would play with her privates to keep his privates
hardened

She begs for pardon, as her lips were muffled
He whispered keep this secret or you will be in so much
trouble
As tears drip from here eyes down to her nasal passages
As memory banks recollect mental baggage
The reality is she has no hiding places
Tears well up in her eyes as her body faces
New traces for her portraits

She tells her mommy he harm me, she doesn't believe her
poor kid
She picked orchids of "he loves me ,he loves me not" kisses
her eardrum

She believes his pleas, which eases her fear some
I can hear teardrops from this good girl, gone bad
So I switch my Bic on this script, grab my pad
Her song had a twisted humming section
Her mommy's men fiddled as they dibbled their little erection
In her direction, shall we list her as a casualty of war? Hell no
Tears drain and stain her face til she's rotten to the core
She forgot to keep score of these encounters
From all of her mom's men friends who would mount her
For bedroom counters, but her mother does not notice
She's so blind to find a man she loses focus
Baby feels hopeless as now all men are the enemy
She is the epitome of a girl who feels no empathy
She feels no sympathy for the youth she once had
Although her tears tell a different story that she wants so bad
She wants her dad, but he was nowhere to protect her
She screams out for mommy, but that woman only neglects her
She deflects her disgrace as misplaced hate
Tried to find her happy place to replace what this place takes
Grave mistakes as she trades love for pain.

A skewed point of view for she only knows what love was
His glove tugs at her teeny, tiny opening
Her will is broken, but she adopts new skills for coping
Hoping that someday this monster will leave her room
Her temple is now her tomb, but now there's baby in her womb
She soon will berth a child spawn from demon seed
She tastes her hate for she would rather see men bleed
We men need to protect her from this twisted mister
In nine months she will give birth to her twisted sister...

Through Her Eyes She Seen Danger And Pain

She was all
Alone in the bathroom scrubbing all clean
She needs to know why and what did it mean.
Was it just that she was in the wrong place?
To have to cope with feeling disgrace.
She was just walking home like she would any day
She had considered going a different way.
But for fear of being hurt she took the shortest path
Not knowing she would become his cruel laugh.
The white van she saw but she tried to go round it
He came out of nowhere and pulled her to sit
Inside his van where no one could see
She hates to tell us what happened to her.
The things that he did are beyond belief
And to be here in my bathroom is such a relief.
She thought he would kill her as he took what he did
She was only 13... Just a little kid
He took from her that precious thing
He took her virginity and dirt came within.
She was scared and so worried of what he would do
She just prayed and waited for the time to be through.
He threw her out as he finished his work
Telling her she was horrid and had just been his perk.
She ran all the way home and climbed into her bath
Hearing that sound as she ran from ... his laugh.
This can happen to anyone at any given time
Know where your kids are protect them
So that this doesn't happen to them
Please.

Children with no voice
Pt. 1

A mother leaves her kids at her parents house
While she goes off to work.
She kisses her 2 yrs old and 6 months old on the head
And says: mommy loves you see you later.
Grand parents say be safe baby driving to work
You know the road has drunken jerks.
Grandpa reads a bed time story to the grand kids
Little babies drift of to sleep lying in bed right next to grandma
Few hours went by then and event that would change there family
Forever happen
Bang, bang, bang shots rang out
Grandpa ran in to the bed room to tell family to duck on the floor
He could here foot steps running away from the house
Grandma clenching the babies but only one was crying
She screams in horror becuz her 2 yr old grand baby was dying
Struck suddenly in the head
The grandpa screamin' not my baby
She can't be dead
The grandma looking in pain all out distraught
But while she holding the 6 month old she seen he had be shot
911 was called the paramedics and firemen and cops all were there
With the look of unbelief and despair
The 2yr old died before help could arrive now the question
Will the 6 month old survive?

The police notified the mother of her lost
She drops knees screaming in agony
Oh noooo not my baby
You got the wrong mother or something
They mention the kids name she passed out
Rush to the same hospital no doubt
Mother sees the
6 month old hooked to ventilation tubes
Grandpa praying to god looking confuses
The men who shot the kids were on the loose
They hid from sight for about 4 months they were on the run
They thought the coast was clear hanging with homies drinking beer
Then a mistake was made that lead a capture

In their drunken state they got into a fight
and the cops were called... People scattered and were screaming they have guns
run and hide...
Shots rang out once again there was more anger in the air
People ducking and diving in lieu of fear
The cops arrived and to their surprise gun shots
Still rang out through the thickness in the air
people on the ground crawling trying to keep from being hit by stray bullets
the cops got down behind their cars and yelled put down
your weapons or we will open fire of course the men said
f*** the police and started to shoot
One telling the other cover while they grab guns and loot
And realized that they had made a bad decision...
The cops finally ended the shoot out with all suspects alive but wounded.

A cops was staring at one of the suspect...told the detective that
Their guns should be taken and sent to ballistics and sure enough theses were the same guns that shot and killed the 2 yr old and shot the 6 month old...
These men were questioned and they didn't know that the cops were still looking into this case they thought they were in the clear.... But when the cops questioned them about the shooting they were shocked and tried to deny it...
But god doesn't like ugly so they couldn't hide it.
But one of the guys couldn't keep his guilt and shame from coming to the surface...
So he yell we didn't mean to hit them kids
A tear ran down his face as his pain lead to pure disgrace
Violence in our community's really must end
Before another child life is cut down before it begin
Justice is not true
Since a little girl life ended at 2
She could been a doctor, lawyer, business woman, or president
For a kid who no has no voice to make her choice.
The criminals were all sentenced to 2 life sentences for this crime...
So when oh when will violence of any kind be eradicated in its time

ReeCee

ReeCee

ReeCee is a copy-editor by trade and as well as a poetic activist. She has been writing poetry since the age of four & has been doing performance poetry/spoken word since 1995.

She has been published in a number of magazines and new including the Oubache and The Illinoisan. Additionally, she had had her work published in two anthologies "Bullying Awareness" and "A Gathering of Words: Poetry and Commentary For Trayvon Martin."

ReeCee's own personal book of poetry, prose & photography entitled "Fishing In Winter" is scheduled for release in May 2014.

She is a mother, artist, founder of Weekend Angels (a community outreach organization for families in Southern Illinois) as well as a volunteer at various homeless, lgbt and womens shelters.

ReeCee can be booked at ree_cee@ymail.com or reached at and (618)204-9809.

http://www.facebook.com/reecee72

For Hannah

Oh, Hannah,
Dearest Hannah,
blessed was your fire/
stoked though
feet of eight/
darkened block/
snuffed flame
sealed your
unconscionable fate.

I inhale the soot
which marked the spot
where once your
hands held paper.

Your splintered pencil
wrote of faith and country,
love and purpose
and I choke from the
breadth of their
enmity towards your innocence.

The sediment grows thick
with apparitions
for whom vindication
has not come, as
I struggle with breaths
acidic from decades of decay.

I am reduced to travailing,
as my lungs, my heart
digest the stench
of horrors you endured.
I want to mourn for you

with peace and reverence,
but am filled with anger
that young poet so gentle
was made martyr.

They caged you,
though could not constrict your spirit.
They beat you,
though each hit only served to remind you were still
breathing.
After grown men had torn into your youthful flesh,
punishing your temple for simply being Jewish,

you faltered only for fleeting moments
before again taking in hand pencil
to write again of blessings and hope.

When they knew finally
they could not break you,
they stood you without benefit of mercy,
no counsel, no marches,
no chance for reprieve
no final countdown
no media,
ns you kneeled
before uniformed soldiers/
shot you like thief,
like vagrant/
young girl at war,
unable to grasp
the impact of your existence.

In those last days of
dolor and muck,
wash and ascendance,
what name did you call
but Mother, Dearest Mother,

what God acknowledged you
Daughter, Faithful Daughter.

No calvary sky darkened/
connect undone/
words not heard,
while execution
fulfilled their plan.

Who came for you,
who came for you
while your Hebrew pen
grew lonesome
for your hand?
Did no one think to aide
those decedents
who now grieve
for never having read
what more you had to say?

Who failed to rescue you,
who WAS it, Hannah?
What man lacked a sense of humanity

and let your worn shoes
be stripped from
weary ankles,
after you paced in circles,
gazing upwards towards
Adonai and Mother?

Did no one come
while ashen tears
fell upon the
blemished face of man?

Who comes for us all,
when we give life for
mission, exchange
sanctuary for mortuary?
Who will rescue OUR words,
who will hear OUR pleas
for love, for peace,
what name will
WE call, but Mother,
Dearest Mother/
when the soot
fills our lungs and our
pens write no more?
Will no one come, Hannah?
Will no one come
for us as
no one
did for you?

Hannah Senesh (July 17, 1921 – November 7, 1944)

Fishing In Winter

Muddy worm held between two fingers
and our giggles carried like the wind across
the pond waters before us.

"If I catch a fish, I'm letting it go,"
I said with mocked defiance to my sister,
two years younger
but older than her days of calendar.

"I can't kill the worm either,
you'll have to do it."

Taking the wriggling thing from me
and laying it out flat in her hand,
we both stared transfixed
as it balled up.

"He wants to be free, I think."
She looked with intent towards the water,
tears in eyes not spilling over.

Shivers from breezes not external shook us both,
as dusk held off
for our decision.

Minutes passed,
while God turned his indulgent gaze
away from us,
though briefly.

Our eyes watched the movement of a turtle
slowly climbing atop a felled sapling.

"We could drown ourselves here
and no one would look for us,"
her voice barely audible.

The worm shrunken atop the lines of her palm
rolled slightly.

"Ok, but let's let him go first, please."
This said twice,
as I thought the lack of response
reflected her not hearing my whisper.

Nervously,
I looked then over rounded shoulder
towards the house I knew to
be deserted.

She kneeled down upon
sunken footsteps freshly made
and set the worm
gently into one of the tracks.

"It's too cold to drown today, Sis,
so we'll wait until it's warmer, ok?"
she rhetorically asked,
without need of answer.

Helping her up from the ground,
we walked together,
arms linked in solidarity.

Trudging through tall grasses,
we headed towards the corn field,
our favorite hiding spot.

We began singing quietly in sibling unison,
"You are my sunshine, my only sunshine,
you make me happy, when skies are gray."

Death postponed needs no explanation,
neither did our pain.

I turned to whistle for our two puppies to follow,
but they stayed there,
resting on the banks,
without ever looking towards us.

Eyes fail to look towards two little girls
in desperate need of being seen.

Long Before That, I Knew Her When

In midnight whispered confessions
she told me her extremities had
never been used for any purpose
other than pleasing men,
but long, long before that,
I knew her when/
knew her smile as though my own reflection,
can even now resurrect the tone inflections
Of the voice that haunts my resting.

Knew her when first she got braids,
twisted them like knots in school boy bellies,
when she winked her rare green eyes
in no specific direction,
she knew her glances left grown men
with erections she could use
to her benefit.

Knew her before her father found proof
Of her indiscretions, so when her footsteps
came in my direction to ask for shelter,
I with no hesitation took her in.

Did not know her womb would fill three times
with clinic rid, unborn children,
did not know her full lips would occupy
both seduction and addiction.

Just knew that she was beautiful and earthy/
thick as red clay pots drying on rocks
soaking up heat without knowing
sun sealed shapes can't know further molding.

Far too many fatherless sons had left the fires
Of desertion smoldering deep within her
And no amount of consoling,
No hours of holding her after night
terrors kept us both awake,
was ever enough to heal her,
for lying deep within were the
echoes of all those men telling her
"bitch, you ain't good enough for love."

But long, long before that, I knew her when
she and I were like young children,
before she was too far gone
and I was too far away
To wrap my arms around her quickly shrinking frame.

Before I could convince her
That her value was in more than hips and contorted legs.
Was worth more than boots and heroin packs,
More than riddled tracks which littered her battered, sunken skin.
Before I could empower her with truth and fact
She fell back
inward.

So it should have come as no surprise when her mother
called late one night and said "baby, I'm real sorry to call
you late like this, but the police think they have her
body down at the morgue and since it's been
two years since last I seen my girl, I was
hoping you could come down
to the police station
and possibly

help me
identify
her
body.

As they pulled the sheet back off her head,
it just reminded me of all those nights she'd
laid beside me in bed, sharing her utopian dream
of one day growing old with me.

I wanted to scream out, "Please, God,
do not take her from me!!! Not yet, please, just not yet."
Yet the pain constricted my breathing,
so I was only able to say four words:
"Yes sir, that's her."

But long, long before that,
I knew her when
and I loved her.

Declaration of War, Securing The Peace

Peace does not come as a result of silence.
Sometimes holding your tongue
serves only the purpose of choking yourself.
Swallowing on words unsaid and gagging
from the thickness of suffering/
with taste of mud and grit of sand,
the past, rotten like fruit left out to spoil
in hot rays of sunshine,
which give life
yet boil
blisters upon the albino skin
of whitewashed histories.

Fusion ignites as hate darkens eyes
like pigmentation gone awry,
looking out from muted faces/
lips closed while the mind races
without action.

Sermons are to be preached
even if it is only to mirrored glasses.
Looking in your eyes and
Seeing there one who was victimized,
No longer accepting blame
or giving out passes
to those who trespassed
against you for their own pleasure.

So you pour salts steadily into
wounds to remind you
of pains purposely inflicted,
refusing to bury secrets,
or let your voice be constricted.

Closing off breaths of fresh air
while behind the pigmentation
of dark iris your eyes stare
out at a world which doled out harm,
like garbage piled deep in landfill farms.

Raising stench like cattle, diseased minds like produce.
Strangling love, preferring to breed abuse,
fertilizing emotional death like flowers which bloom.

So today, I take pack power from you,
though the rain is too acidic to quench my thirst
I declare war so as to preserve life,
force my voice to erupt like seeds from the Earth/
not gently peeking out
but pushing forth with such voracity
the dirt can not contain it
and if peace and safety
are not properly planted
I will claim them,
with words that can not be stifled/
take aim with vocal armory, shot like rifles.

I won't wait for justice with my tongue tied,
proclamations of happened transgressions
I refuse to hide under blankets of whispers and fear.

So don’t hold your ears near,
As I am prone to scream.

I refuse to let the refuse which was bequeathed to me
lie buried inside quietly.

Yes, I vow to declare war for the purpose of peace/
Boisterously,
So that others like me
will not
have to suffer
alone,
silently.

Shannon Stanton

Shannon Stanton

My name is Shannon Stanton and I consider myself an artist. I love to write poems and stories about my ever growing personal experiences that have bought me joy, pain and purpose. In the 41 years that i have lived, my most rewarding and valuable gift is the ability to express my feelings and thoughts thru my GOD-given gift of writing. My purpose is to give back what was so freely given to me: the message of hope, freedom and joy through all of my trials and afflictions. After all, what good would my gift be if I'm not willing to share it? My main objective for writing is that GOD uses me as a vessel to bless someone, and that GOD continues to bless us all....real good.

Broken Child

As I look back on my childhood, I see a child was scorn,
It often had me wishing that I never had been born.
I harbor a lot of memories I wish I'd never kept,
Flash backs of a broken hearted child crying out for help.
Always looking for attention because my father wasn't there,
I was a loner that always thought that no one really cared.
I had to deal with beatings and I was far too young to fight,
Always pointed out for all my wrongs and nothing I did right.
My childhood was a stopping point, I never had a chance to start,
I learned to be a broken child, and that really broke my heart.

I am not 7

I hope this poem releases me, I am not 7.
More than anything else, i just want to be free, I am not 7.
Just because my innocence was taken away, I am not 7.
Doesn't mean I have to re-live it each day, I am not 7.
I sometimes dwell on what was lost, I am not 7.
I must understand that it wasn't my fault, I am not 7.
Even though I'm a victim to what has been done, I am not 7.
I understand now I'm not the only one, I am not 7.
I realize now that I had no control, I am not 7.
It's time to release the pain I still hold, I am not 7.
I refuse to let guilt consume me any longer, I am not 7.
What didn't kill me has made me stronger, I am not 7.
I refuse to be angry and put on a mask, I am not 7.
I am a survivor of my past, I am not 7.
I refuse to use my past a a crutch, I am not 7.
It's time for the little girl to finally grow up, I am not 7.

Alone

When I chose the pressure over the peer, I didn't know what I'd done,
I didn't know the pain and misery that was soon to come.
So young and naive that at the time, I didn't know what to do,
I never once considered the hurt I'd put my family through.
I wandered down the road of life without any direction,
And when danger was all around I didn't have any protection.
I looked for love in all the wrong places, and when I made it there,
I was never satisfied with anything, and that got me no where.
Back when I was only a child, I was always scrutinized,
It made me feel so worthless, I was nobody in my own eyes.
Before I knew what happened, all my self-esteem was gone,
Reality hit me and I thought it was best to try to make it all alone.

I remember

I remember being caught in a trap, and no one seemed to care,
I remember the night i forgot to dream and life turned into a nightmare.
I remember when I would sell my soul, just to get some more,
I remember when I had no hope and nothing to live for.
I remember when fear was chasing me, I tried to run and hide,
I remember feeling so empty and numb on the inside.
I remember when I would jump in cars with strangers willing to pay.
I remember when some of them tried to kill me and take my life away.
I remember how I fought and screamed and managed to escape,
I remember trying it all again, I remember being raped.
I remember being homeless and I had no where to go,
I remember being hungry, tired and outside in the cold.
I remember when I thought it couldn't get any worse for me,
I remember when the doctor said, you now have HIV.
I remember being all alone and feeling sorry for myself,
I remember the day I prayed to GOD because I knew that HE would help.
I remember how he fed my soul with positive energy,
And when the world had witnessed the worst, GOD bought out the best in me.
I remember how my life was then and how GOD came and changed it,
I will never forget without GOD on my side, I never would have made it.

Song Lyrics

works by

Where Do The Children Play?
Cat Stevens aka Yusuf Islam

Father And Son
Cat Stevens aka Yusuf Islam

Time In A Bottle
Jim Croce

Cat's In The Cradle
Harry Chapin

Where Do The Children Play?

Cat Stevens aka Yusuf Islam

Well I think it's fine, building jumbo planes.
Or takin' a ride on a cosmic train.
Switch on summer from a slot machine.
Get what you want to if you want,
Cause you can get anything.

I know we've come a long way,
We're changin' day to day,
But tell me,
Where do the children play?

Well you roll on roads over fresh green grass.
For your lorryloads pumping petrol gas.
And you make them long, and you make them tough.
But they just go on and on,
And it seems you can't get off.

Oh, I know we've come a long way,
We're changin' day to day,
But tell me,
Where do the children play?

When you crack the sky, scrapers fill the air.
Will you keep on building higher
Til there's no more room up there?
Will you make us laugh, will you make us cry?
Will you tell us when to live?
Will you tell us when to die?

I know we've come a long way,
We're changin' day to day,
But tell me,
Where do the children play?

http://youtu.be/7a4DCxAi020

Father And Son

Cat Stevens aka Yusuf Islam

Father
It's not time to make a change,
Just relax, take it easy.
You're still young, that's your fault,
There's so much you have to know.
Find a girl, settle down,
If you want you can marry.
Look at me, I am old, but I'm happy.

I was once like you are now, and I know that it's not easy,
To be calm when you've found something going on.
But take your time, think a lot,
Why, think of everything you've got.
For you will still be here tomorrow, but your dreams may not.

Son
How can I try to explain, when I do he turns away again.
It's always been the same, same old story.
From the moment I could talk I was ordered to listen.
Now there's a way and I know that I have to go away.
I know I have to go.

Father
It's not time to make a change,
Just sit down, take it slowly.
You're still young, that's your fault,
There's so much you have to go through.
Find a girl, settle down,
if you want you can marry.
Look at me, I am old, but I'm happy.

Son
All the times that I cried, keeping all the things I knew inside,
It's hard, but it's harder to ignore it.
If they were right, I'd agree, but it's them you know not me.
Now there's a way and I know that I have to go away.
I know I have to go.

http://youtu.be/Q29YR5-t3gg

Time In A Bottle
Jim Croce

If I could save time in a bottle
The first thing that I'd like to do
Is to save every day till eternity passes away
Just to spend them with you

If I could make days last forever
If words could make wishes come true
I'd save every day like a treasure and then
Again, I would spend them with you

But there never seems to be enough time
To do the things you want to do, once you find them
I've looked around enough to know
That you're the one I want to go through time with

If I had a box just for wishes
And dreams that had never come true
The box would be empty, except for the memory of how
They were answered by you

But there never seems to be enough time
To do the things you want to do, once you find them
I've looked around enough to know
That you're the one I want to go through time with

Cat's In The Cradle

Harry Chapin

My child arrived just the other day
He came to the world in the usual way
But there were planes to catch and bills to pay
He learned to walk while I was away
And he was talkin' 'fore I knew it, and as he grew
He'd say "I'm gonna be like you, Dad
You know I'm gonna be like you"

And the cat's in the cradle and the silver spoon
Little boy blue and the man on the moon
When you comin' home, Dad
I don't know when, but we'll get together then
You know we'll have a good time then

My son turned ten just the other day
He said, "Thanks for the ball, Dad, come on let's play
can you teach me to throw", I said "Not today
I got a lot to do", he said, "That's ok
And he walked away but his smile never dimmed
And said, "I'm gonna be like him, yeah
You know I'm gonna be like him"

And the cat's in the cradle and the silver spoon
Little boy blue and the man on the moon
When you comin' home, Dad
I don't know when, but we'll get together then
You know we'll have a good time then

Well, he came from college just the other day
So much like a man I just had to say
"Son, I'm proud of you, can you sit for a while"
He shook his head and said with a smile
"What I'd really like, Dad, is to borrow the car keys
See you later, can I have them please"

And the cat's in the cradle and the silver spoon
Little boy blue and the man on the moon
When you comin' home son
I don't know when, but we'll get together then, Dad
You know we'll have a good time then

I've long since retired, my son's moved away
I called him up just the other day
I said, "I'd like to see you if you don't mind"
He said, "I'd love to, Dad, if I can find the time
You see my new job's a hassle and kids have the flu
But it's sure nice talking to you, Dad
It's been sure nice talking to you"

And as I hung up the phone it occurred to me
He'd grown up just like me
My boy was just like me

And the cat's in the cradle and the silver spoon
Little boy blue and the man in the moon
When you comin' home son
I don't know when, but we'll get together then, Dad
We're gonna have a good time then

http://youtu.be/_QX_1mOMXHo

Other

Anthological

works by

Inner Child Press, ltd.

www.innerchildpress.com

Inner Child Press Anthologies

Inner Child Press Anthologies

Inner Child Press Anthologies

the Year of the Poet

April 2014

The Poetry Posse

Jamie Bond
Gail Weston Shazor
Albert 'Infinite' Carrasco
Siddartha Beth Pierce
Janet P. Caldwell
June 'Bugg' Barefield
Debbie M. Allen
Tony Henninger
Joe DaVerbal Minddancer
Robert Gibbons
Neetu Wali
Shareef Abdur-Rasheed
Kimberly Burnham
William S. Peters, Sr.

Our April Featured Poets

Fahredin Shehu
Martina Reisz Newberry
Justin Blackburn
Monte Smith

celebrating international poetry month

Inner Child Press Anthologies

Inner Child Press

Anthologies

the Year of the Poet

February 2014

violets

The Poetry Posse

Jamie Bond
Gail Weston Shazor
Albert 'Infinite' Carrasco
Siddartha Beth Pierce
Janet P. Caldwell
June 'Bugg' Barefield
Debbie M. Allen
Tony Henninger
Joe DaVerbal Minddancer
Robert Gibbons
Neetu Wali
Shareef Abdur-Rasheed
William S. Peters, Sr.

Our February Features

Teresa E. Gallion & Robert Gibson

The Year of the Poet
January 2014
The Poetry Posse
Jamie Bond
Gail Weston Shazor
Albert 'Infinite' Carrasco
Siddartha Beth Pierce
Janet P. Caldwell
June 'Bugg' Barefield
Debbie M. Allen
Tony Henninger
Joe DaVerbal Minddancer
Robert Gibbons
Neetu Wali
Shareef Abdur-Rasheed
William S. Peters, Sr.
Carnation
Our January Feature
Terri L. Johnson

Inner Child Press
Anthologies

Mandela

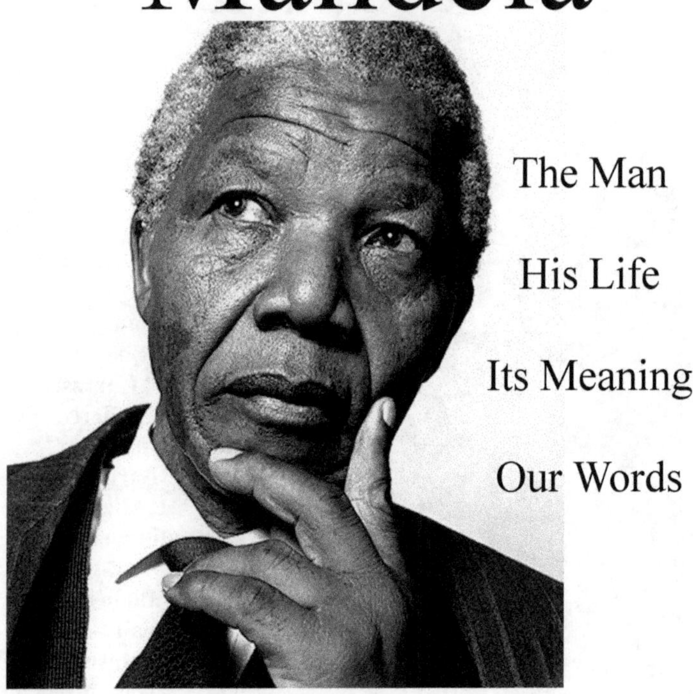

Poetry . . . Commentary & Stories

The Anthological Writers

A GATHERING OF WORDS

POETRY & COMMENTARY
FOR

TRAYVON MARTIN

Inner Child Press Anthologies

Inner Child Press Anthologies

Inner Child Press Anthologies

Inner Child Press Anthologies

Inner Child Press Anthologies

Inner Child Press Anthologies

Inner Child Press Anthologies

a collection of the Voices of Many inspired by …

Monte Smith

Inner Child Press Anthologies

a collection of the Voices of Many inspired by . . .

Monte Smith

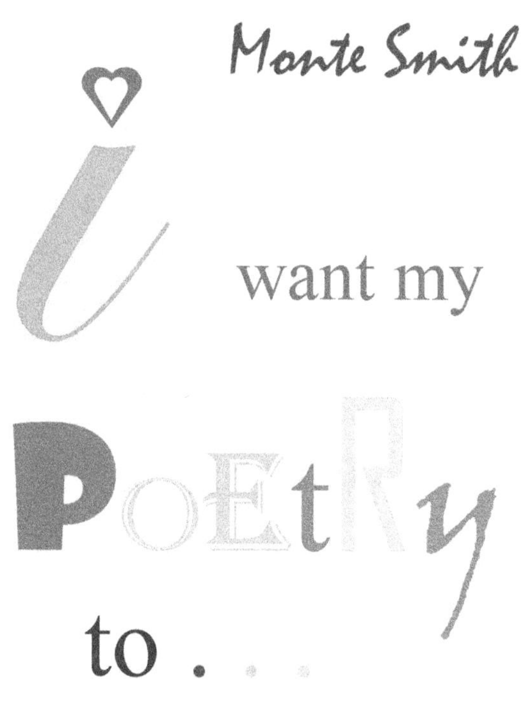

volume II

and there is much, much more !

visit . . .

http://www.innerchildpress.com
/anthologies-sales-special.php

Also check out our Authors and
all the wonderful Books
Available at :

http://www.innerchildpress.com
/the-book-store.php

Inner Child Press Anthologies

www.worldhealingworldpeacepoetry.com

Inner Child Press Anthologies

TEE SHIRTS

&

HATS

SALE

Tee Shirts for Sale

World Healing ~ World Peace

$ 20.00

Small * Med. * Large * XL * XXL

www.worldhealingworldpeacepoetry.com

Anthologies for Sale

$ 22.00

http://www.innerchildpress.com/the-year-of-the-poet.php

Anthologies for Sale

COMBOS

$ 40.00

SMALL * MED. * LARGE * XL * XXL

http://www.innerchildpress.com/the-year-of-the-poet.php

Tee Shirts for Sale

COMBOS

$ 50.00

Small * Med. * Large * XL * XXL

http://www.innerchildpress.com/the-year-of-the-poet.php

Anthologies for Sale

The Year of the Poet

$ 20.00

Small * Med. * Large * XL * XXL

http://www.innerchildpress.com/the-year-of-the-poet.php

This Anthological Publication
is underwritten solely by

Inner Child Press

Inner Child Press is a Publishing Company Founded and Operated by Writers. Our personal publishing experiences provides us an intimate understanding of the sometimes daunting challenges Writers, New and Seasoned may face in the Business of Publishing and Marketing their Creative "Written Work".

For more Information

Inner Child Press

www.innerchildpress.com

FINI

www.ingramcontent.com/pod-product-compliance
Lightning Source LLC
LaVergne TN
LVHW051052080426
835508LV00019B/1829

* 9 7 8 0 6 9 2 2 1 3 2 6 1 *